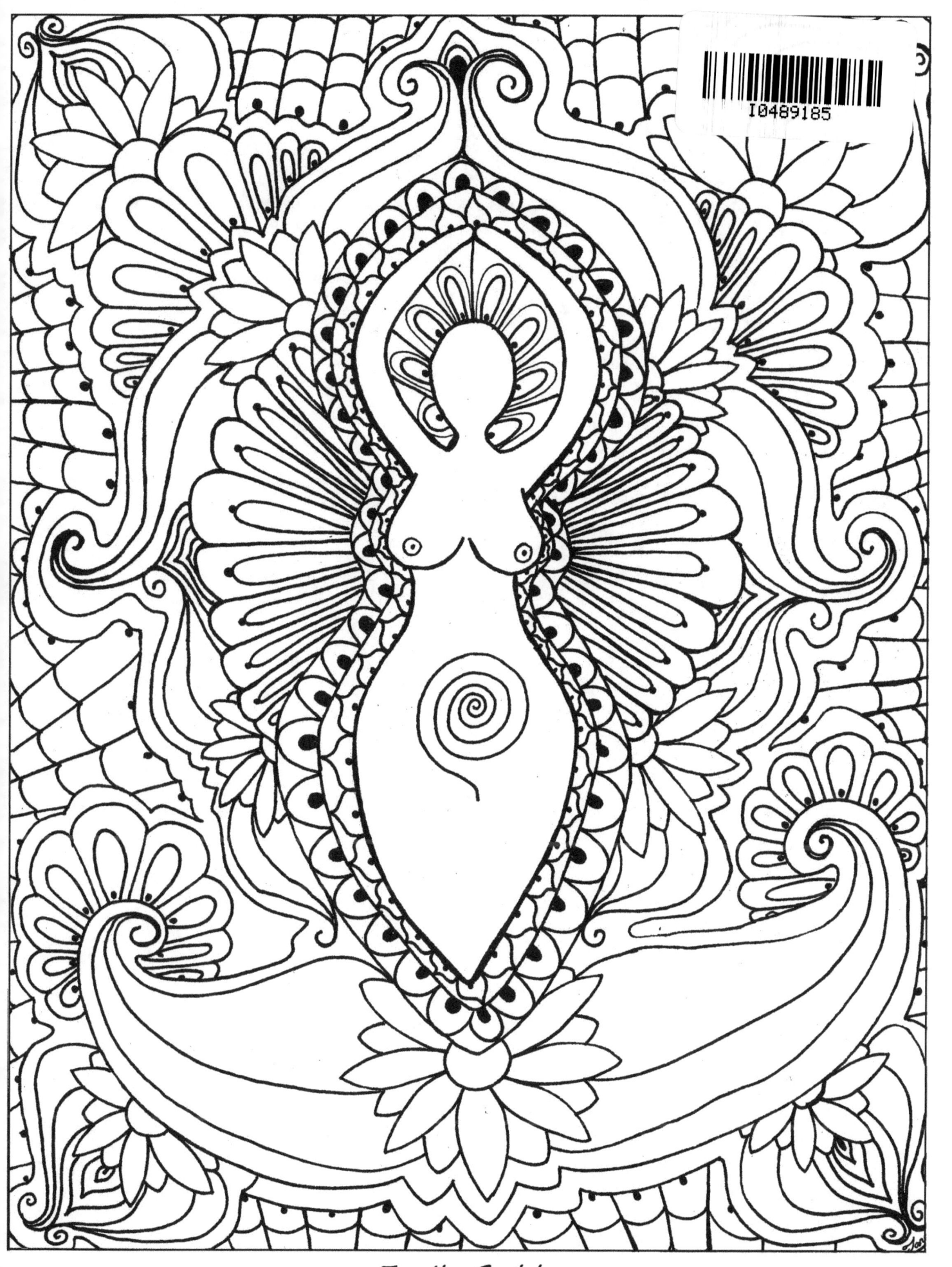

Earth Goddess

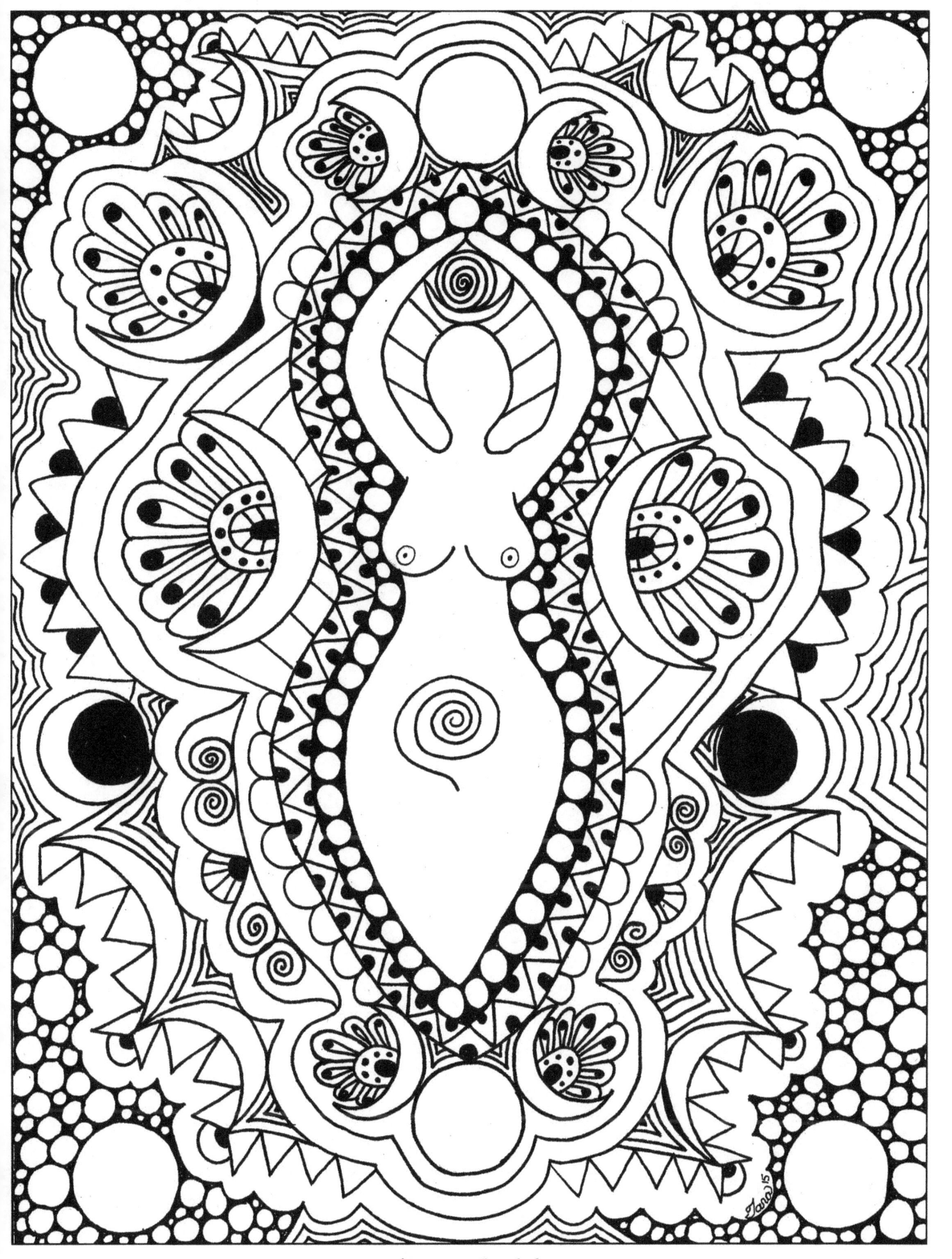

Moon Goddess

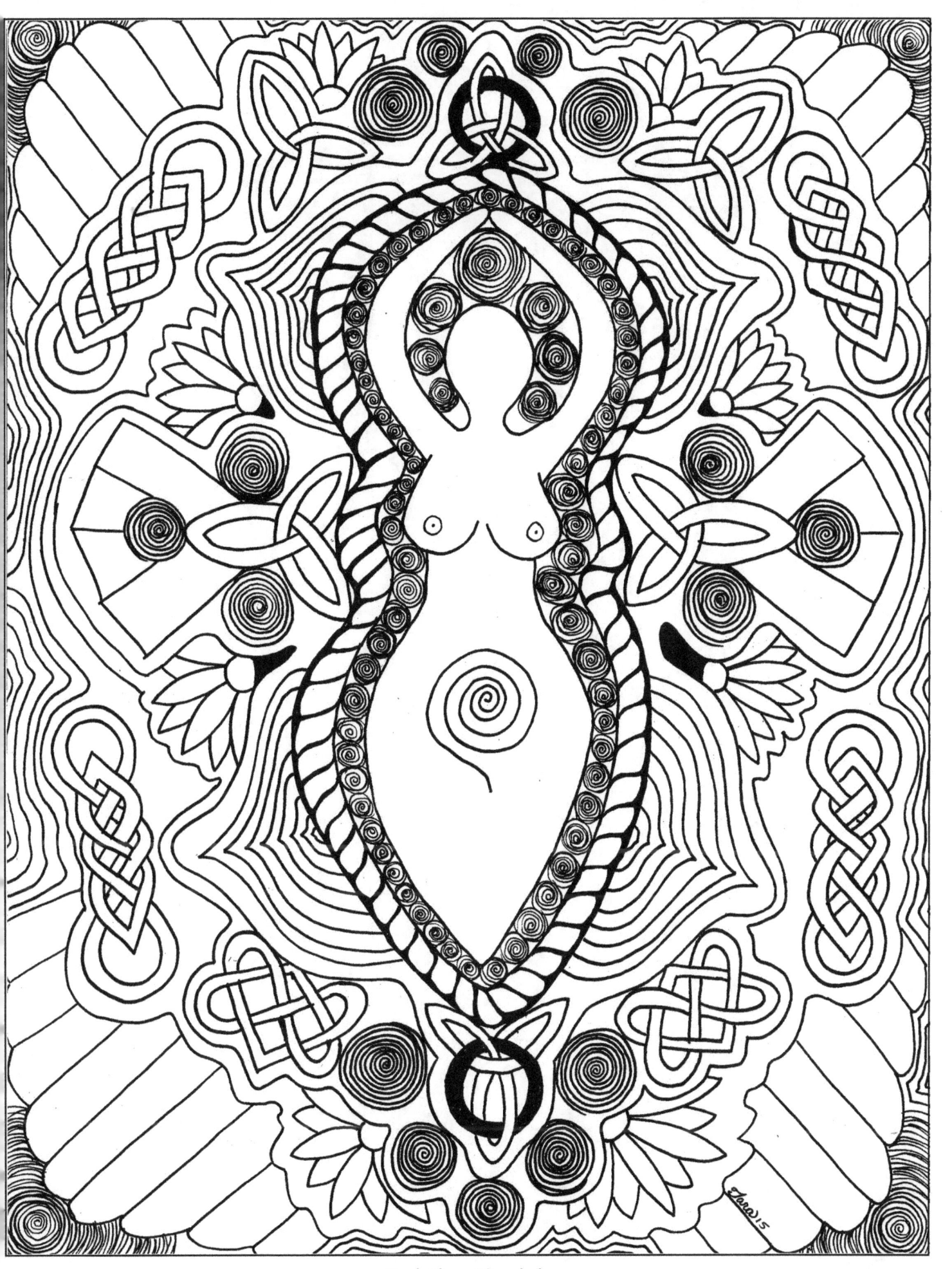

Celtic Goddess

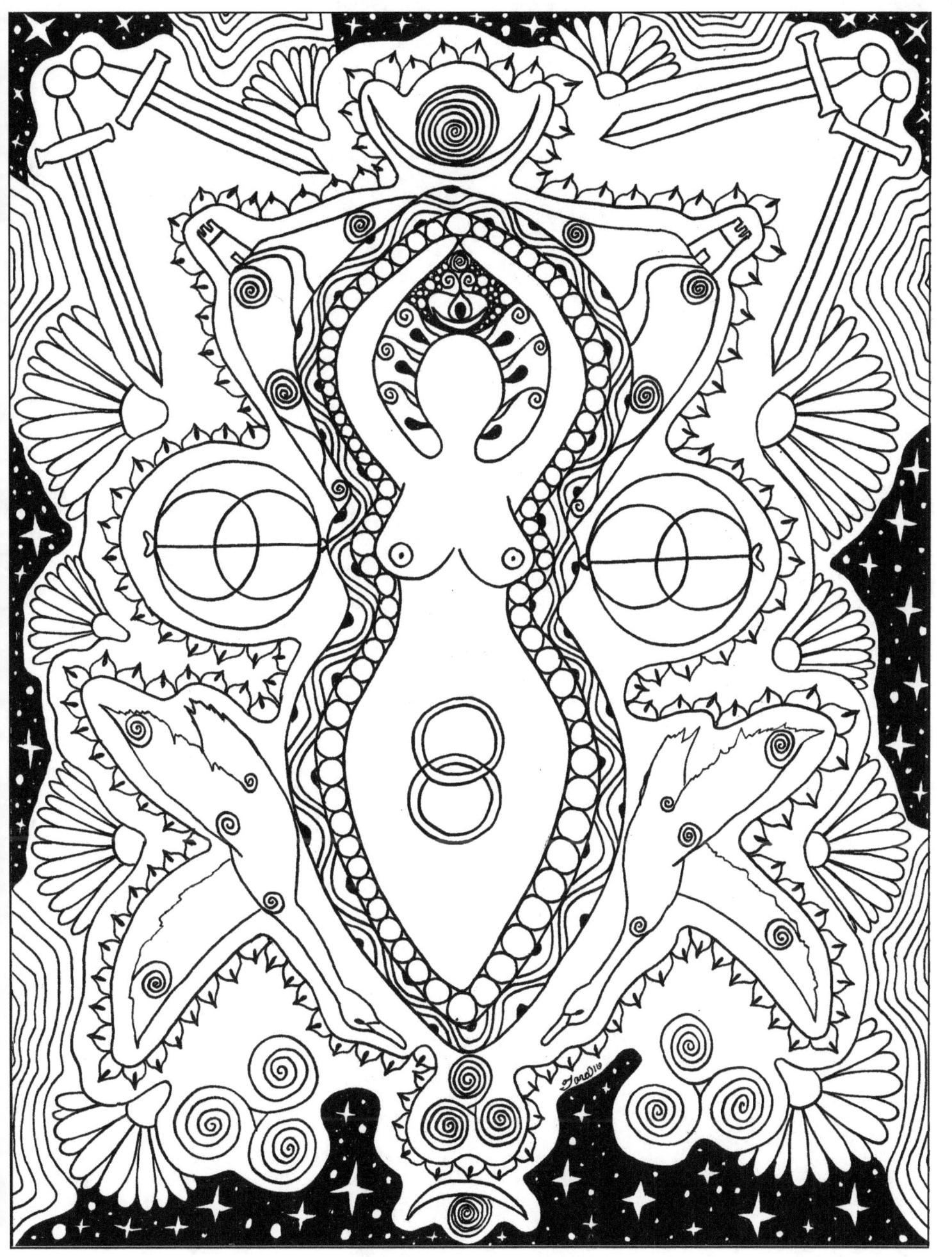

Goddess of Avalon

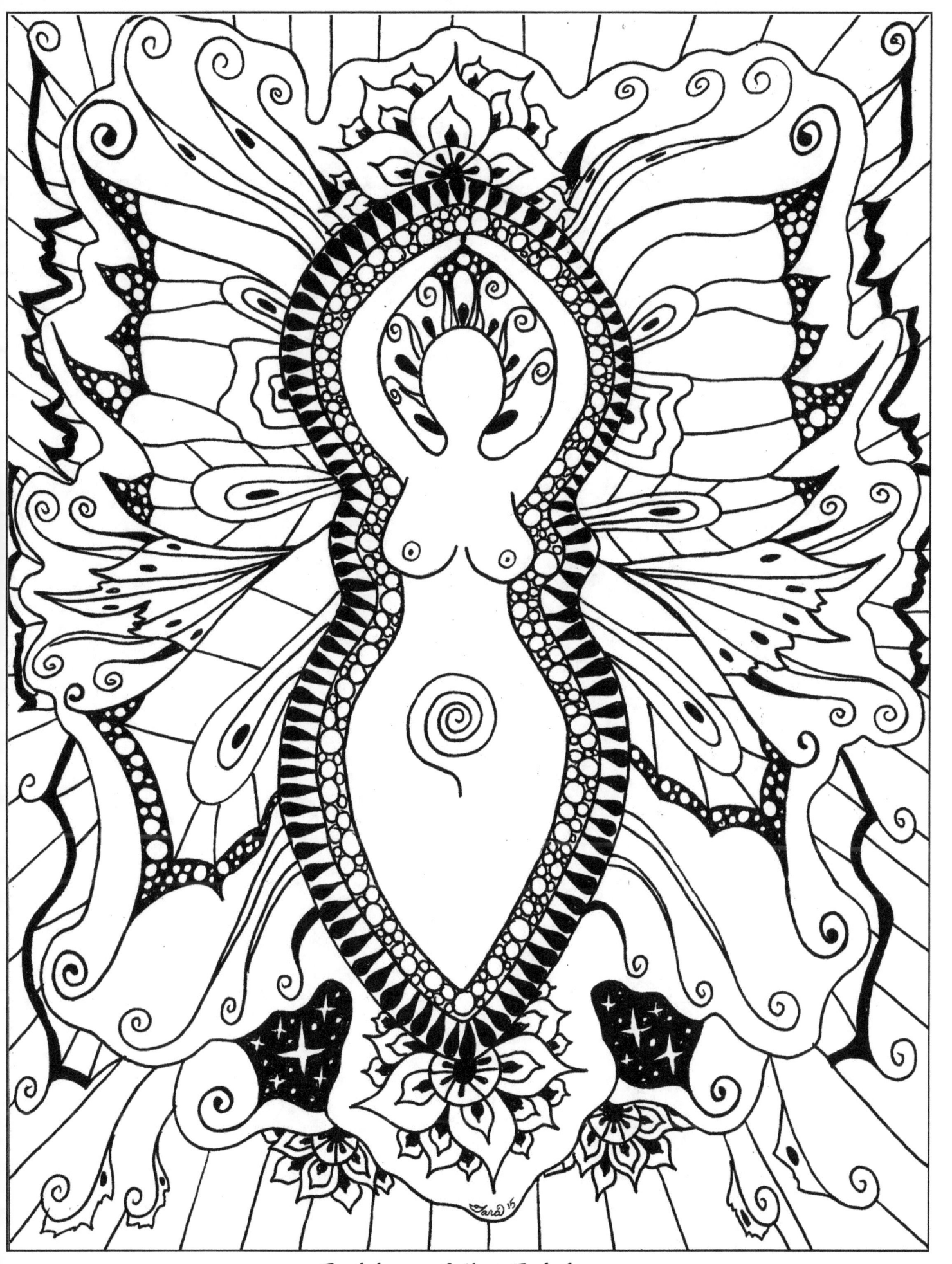

Goddess of the Fairies

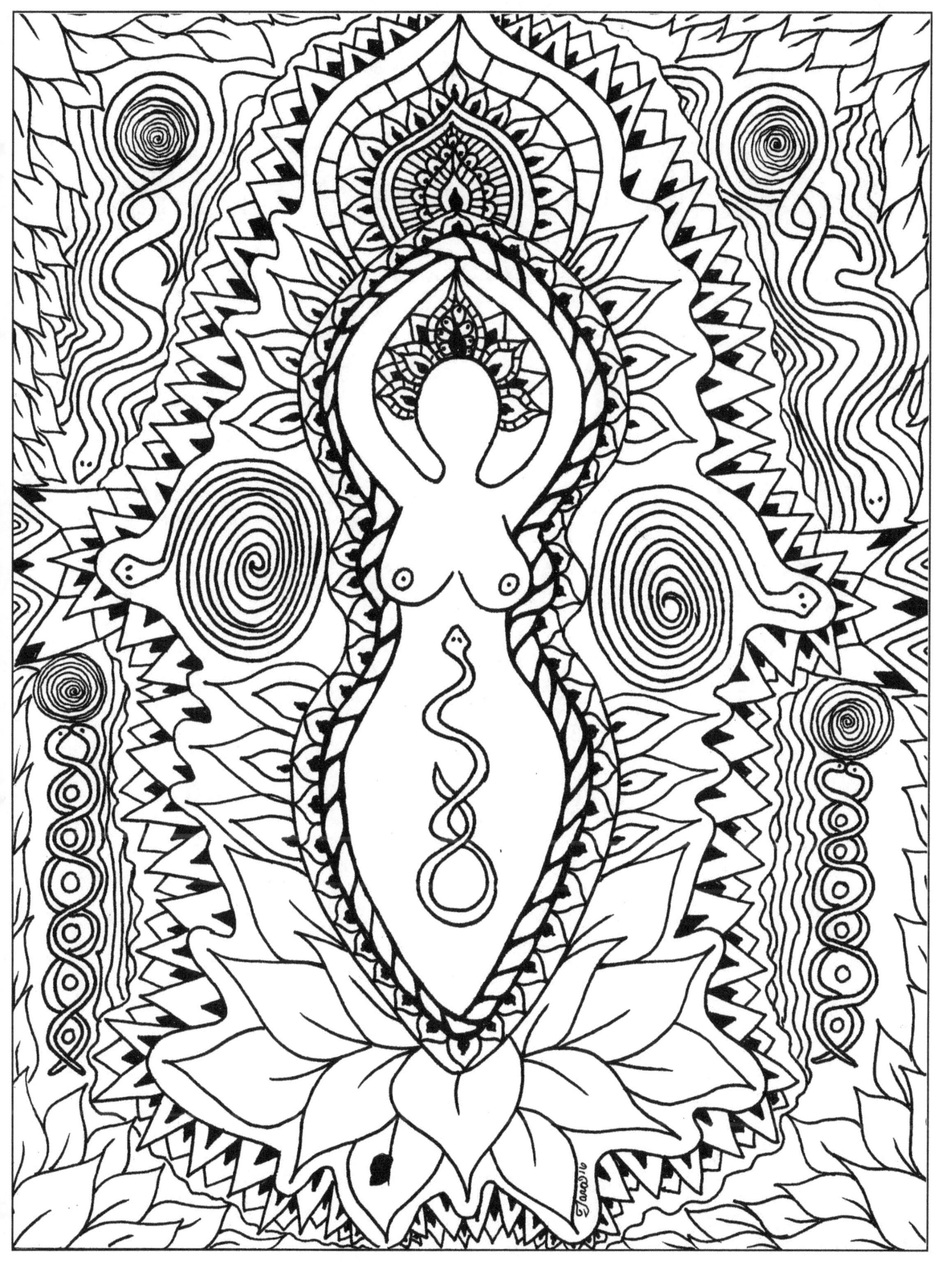

Kundalini Goddess

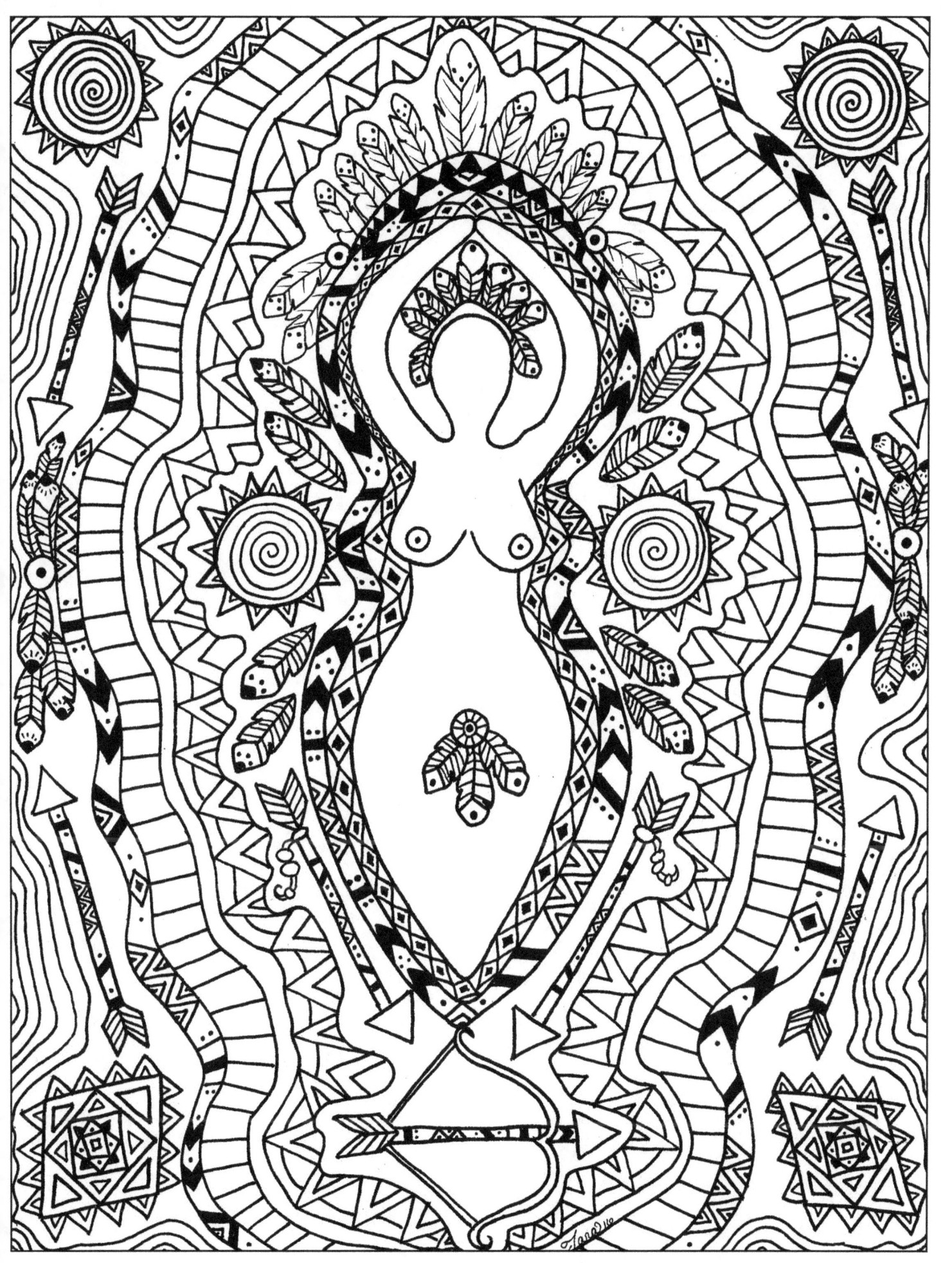

Wild Woman Goddess

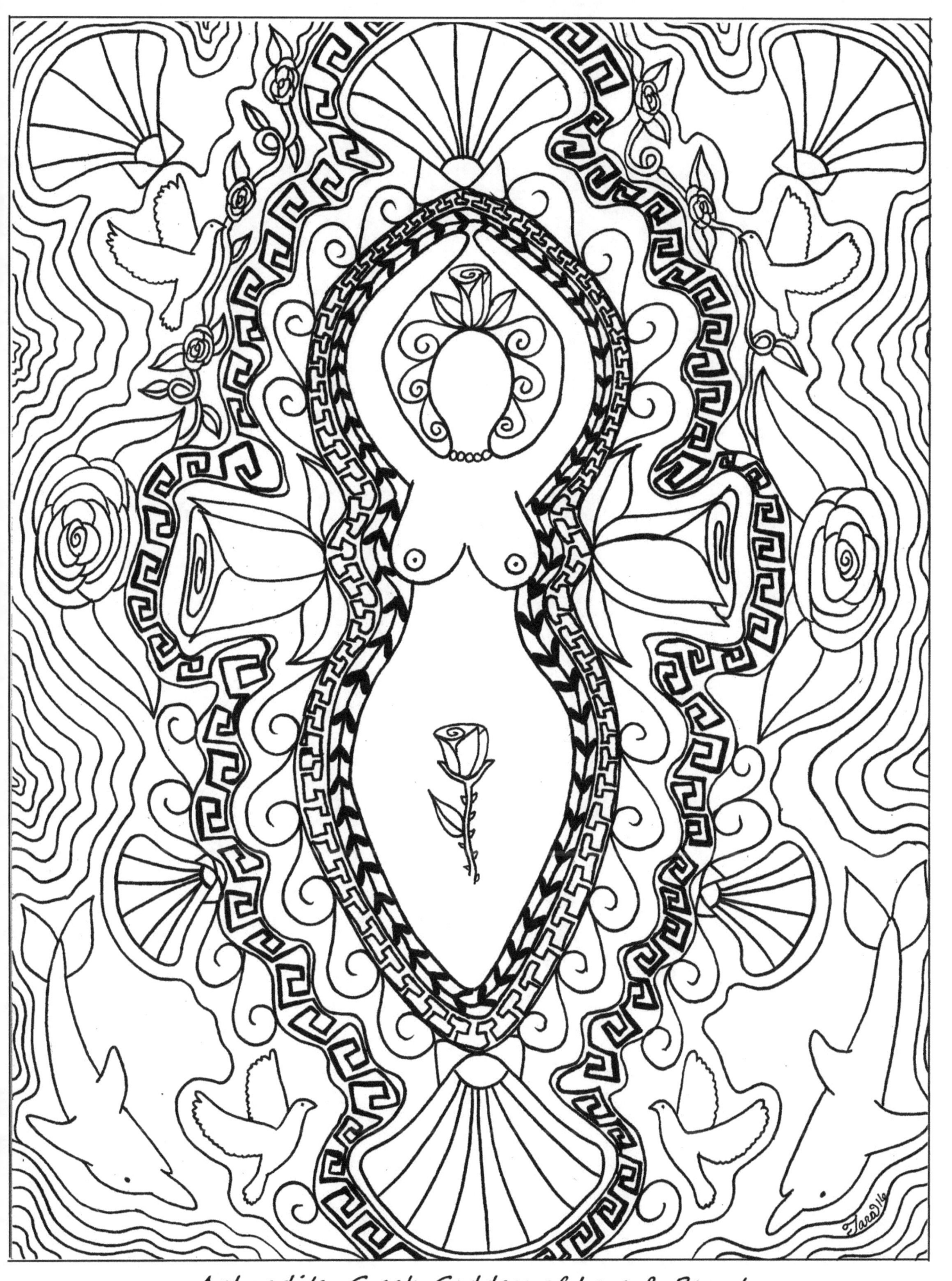

Aphrodite, Greek Goddess of Love & Beauty

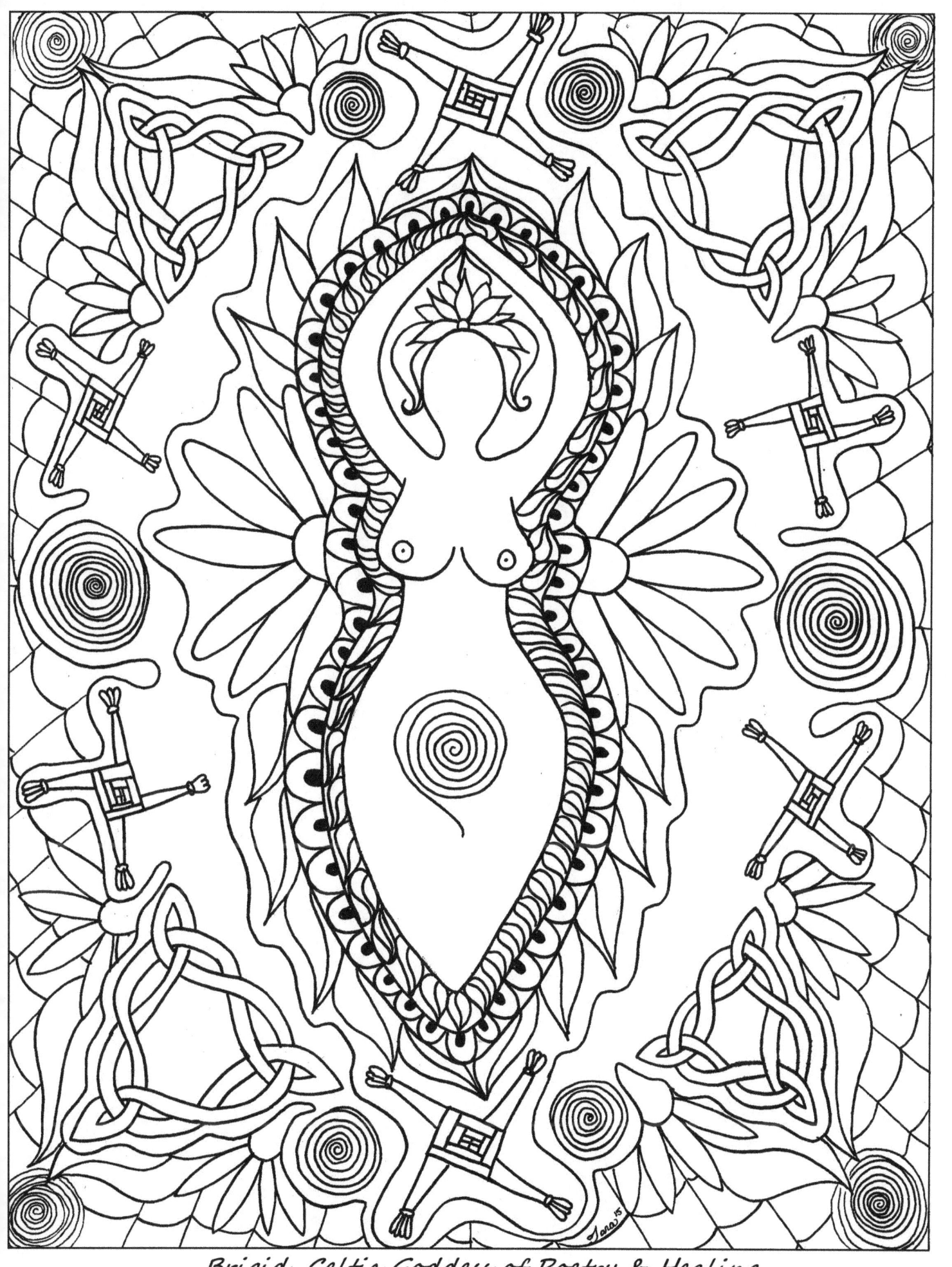

Brigid, Celtic Goddess of Poetry & Healing

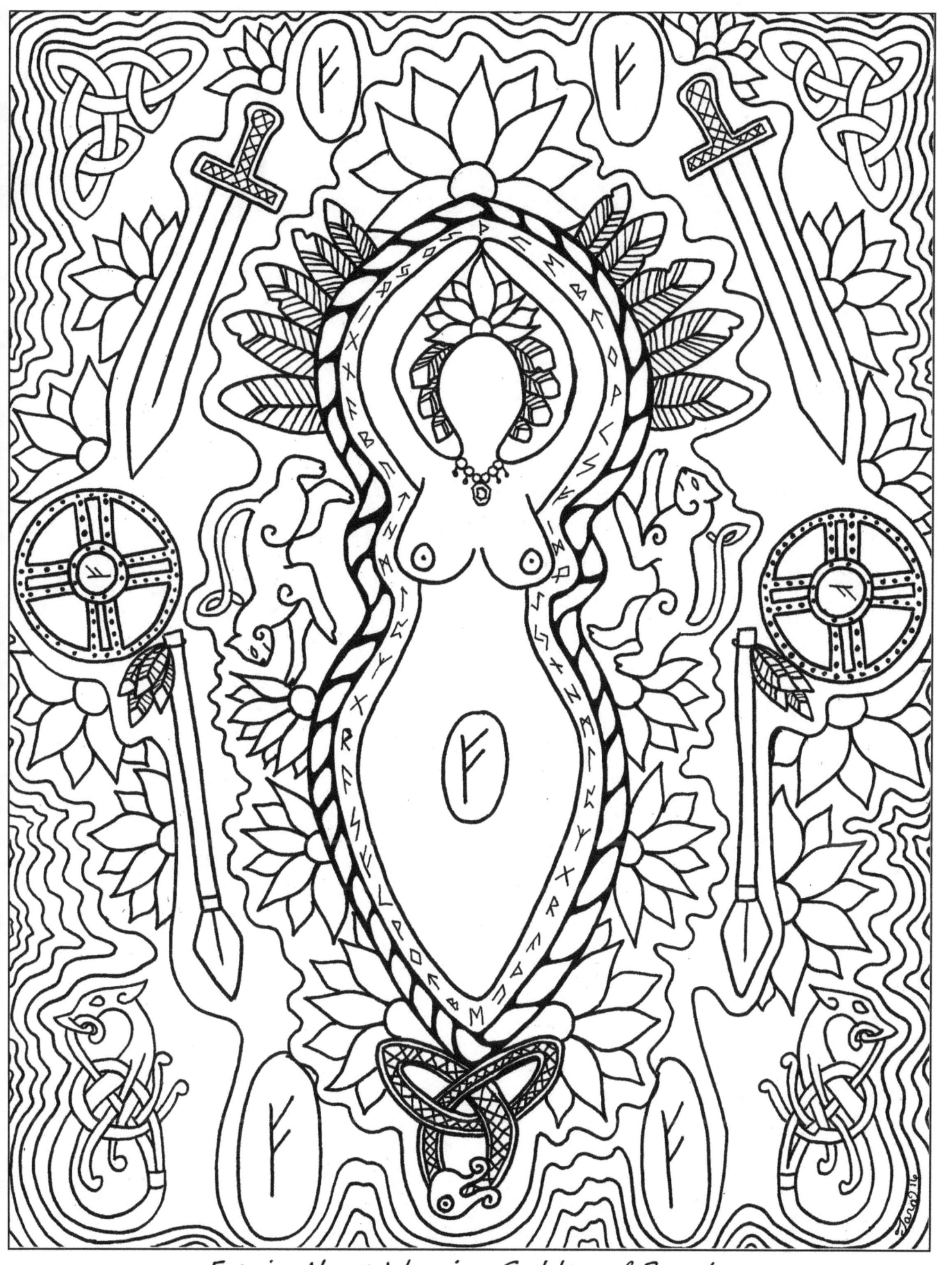

Freyja, Norse Warrior Goddess of Beauty

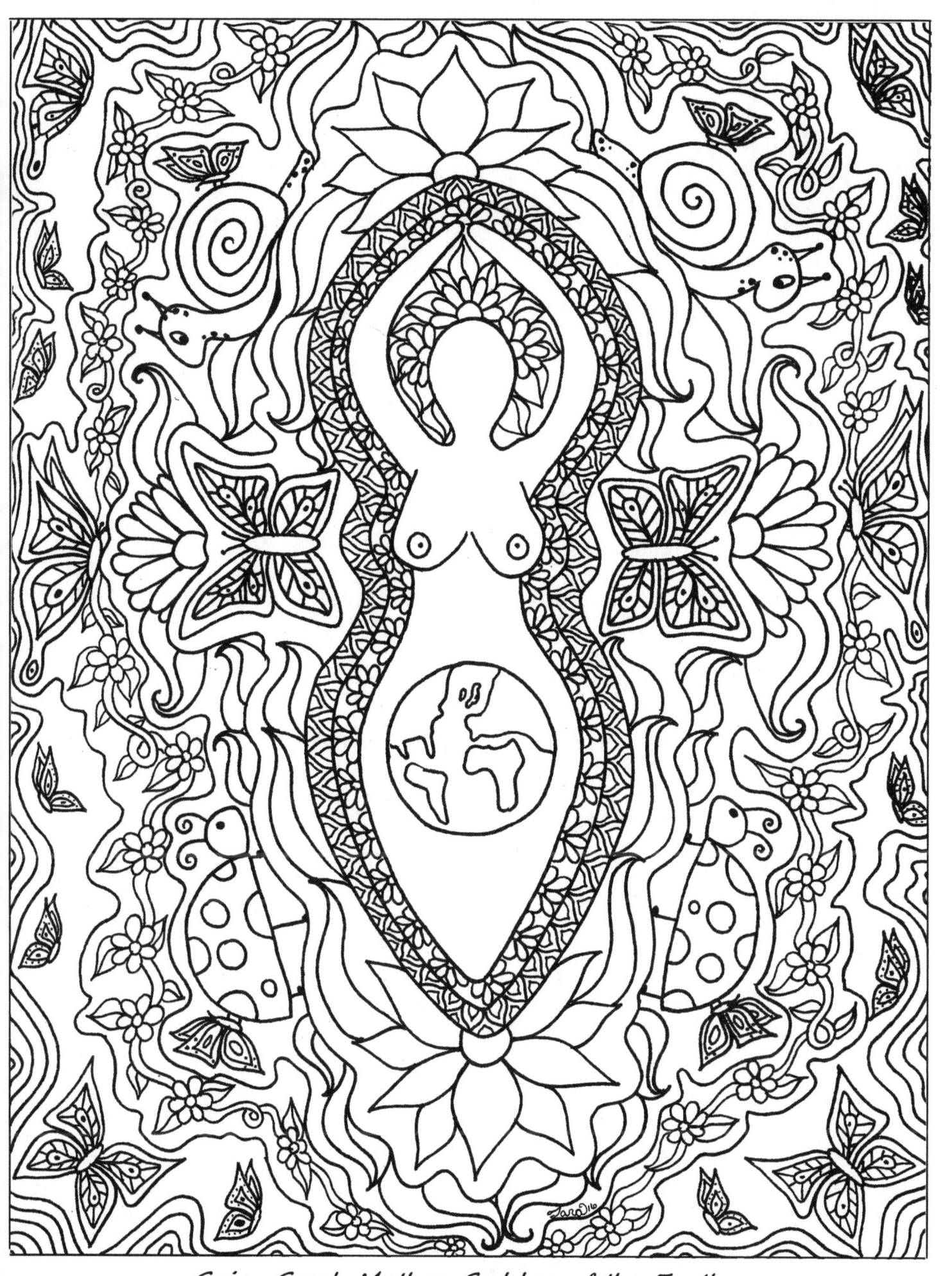

Gaia, Greek Mother Goddess of the Earth

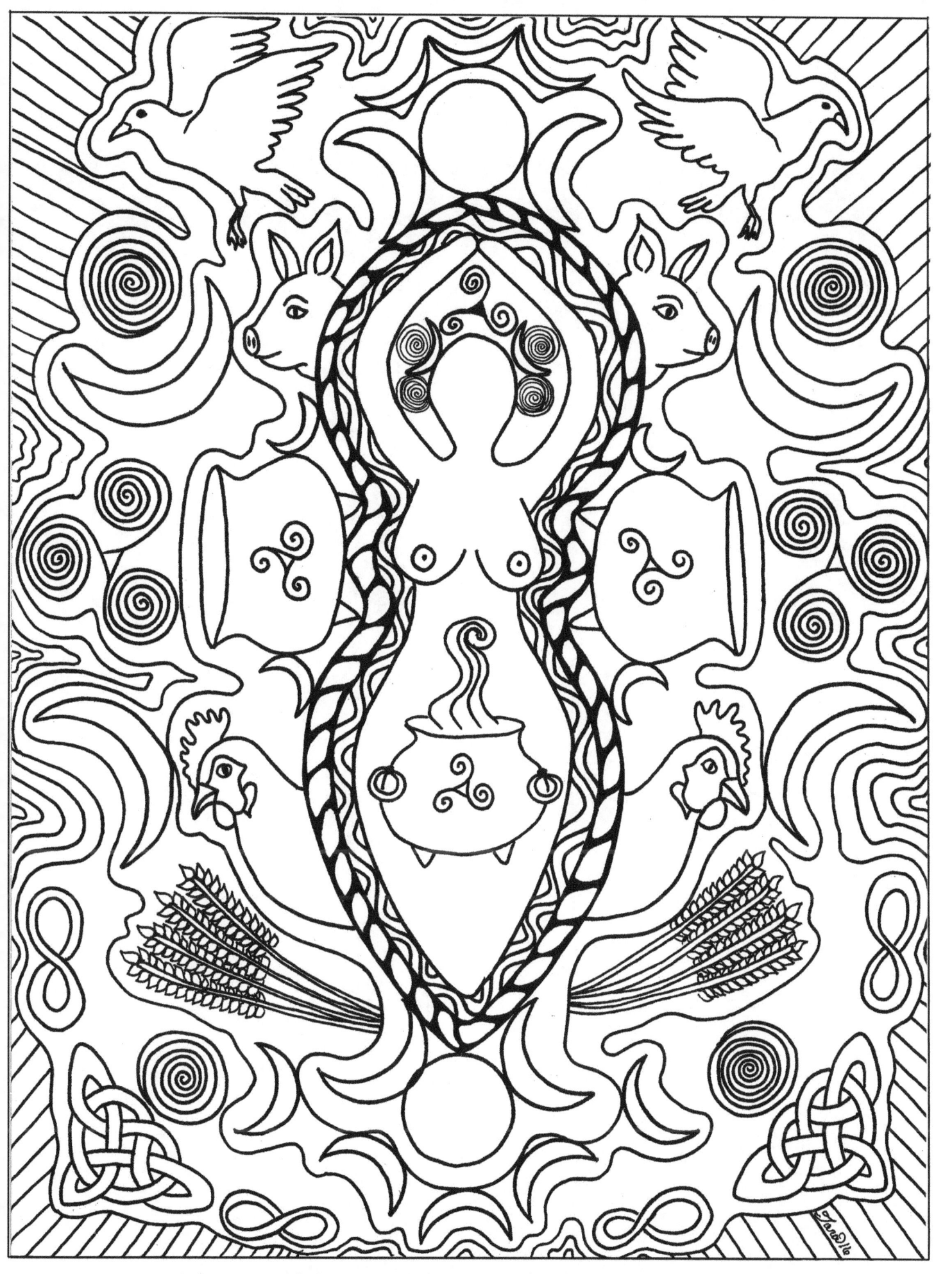

Cerridwen, Welsh Goddess of Magic & Transformation

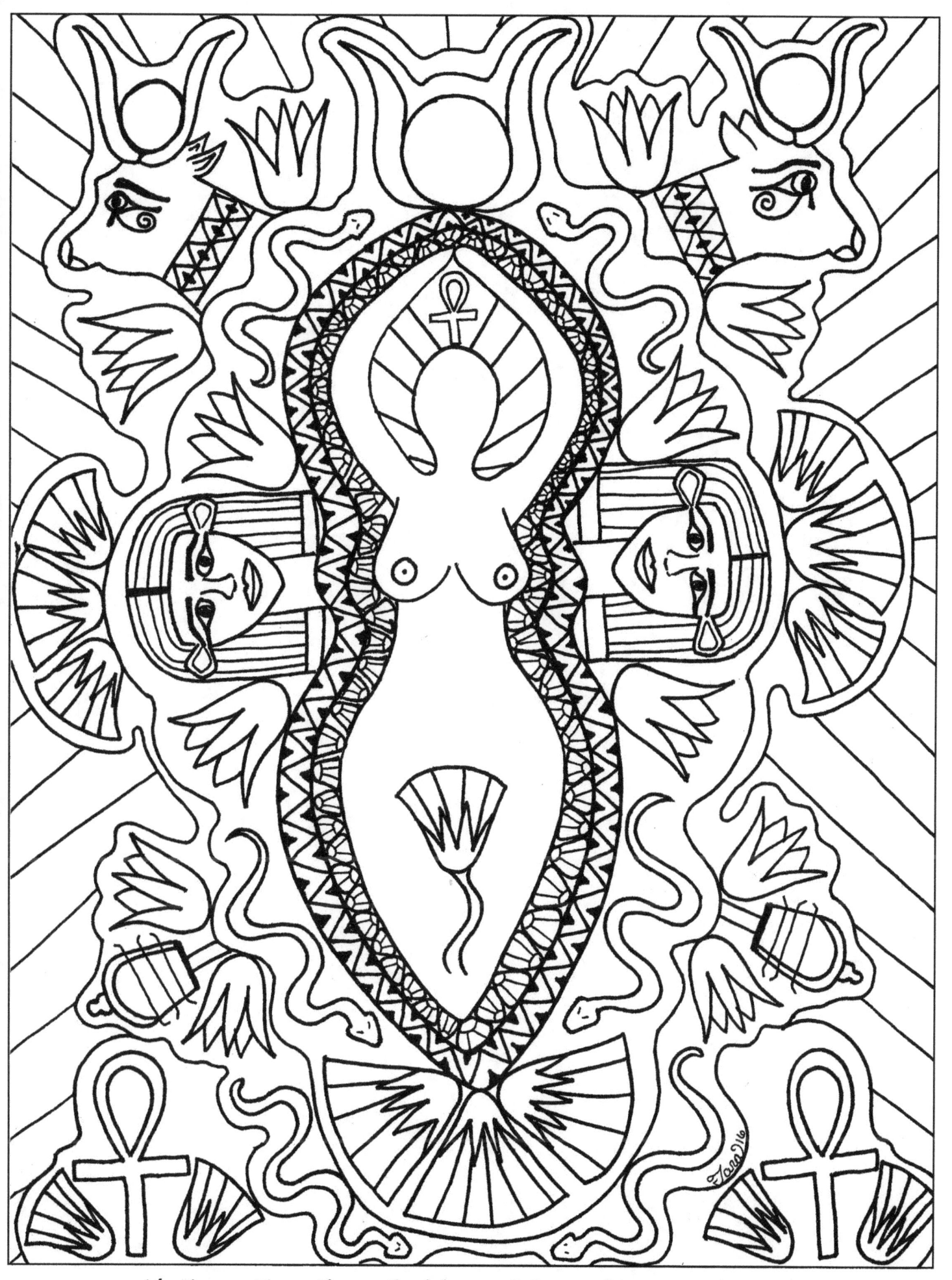

Hathor, Egyptian Goddess of Sacred Dance & Love

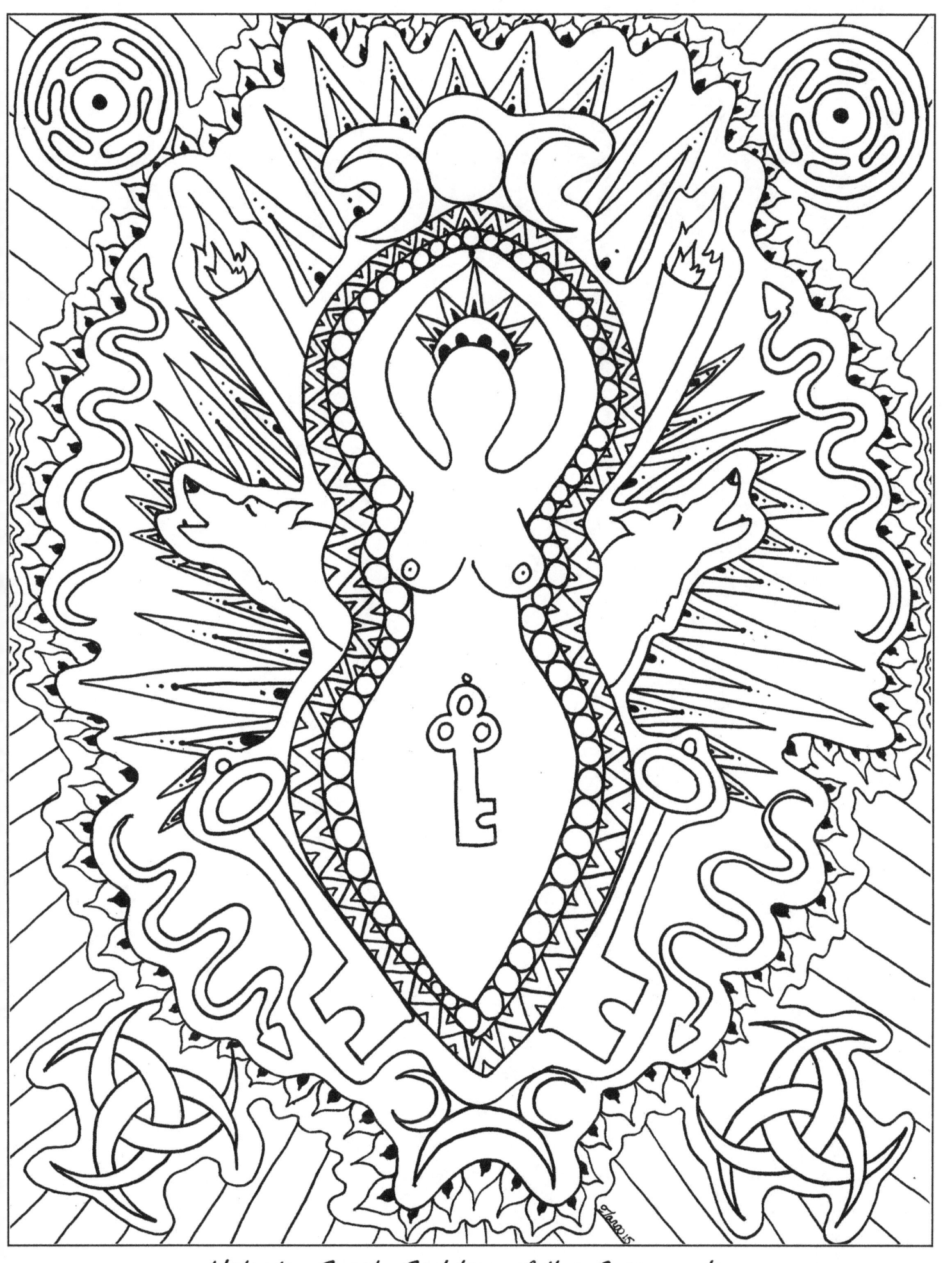

Hekate, Greek Goddess of the Crossroads

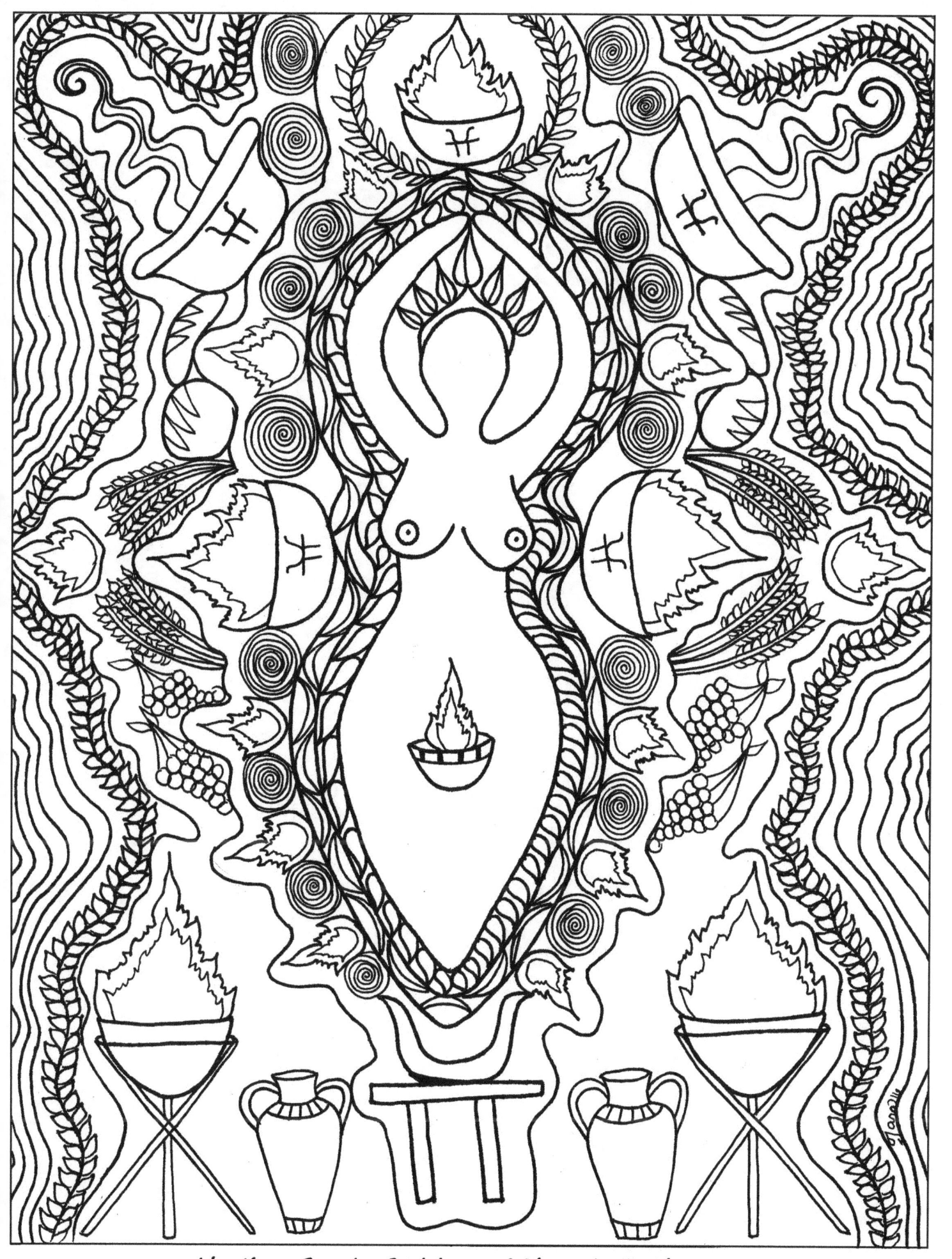

Hestia, Greek Goddess of Hearth & Home

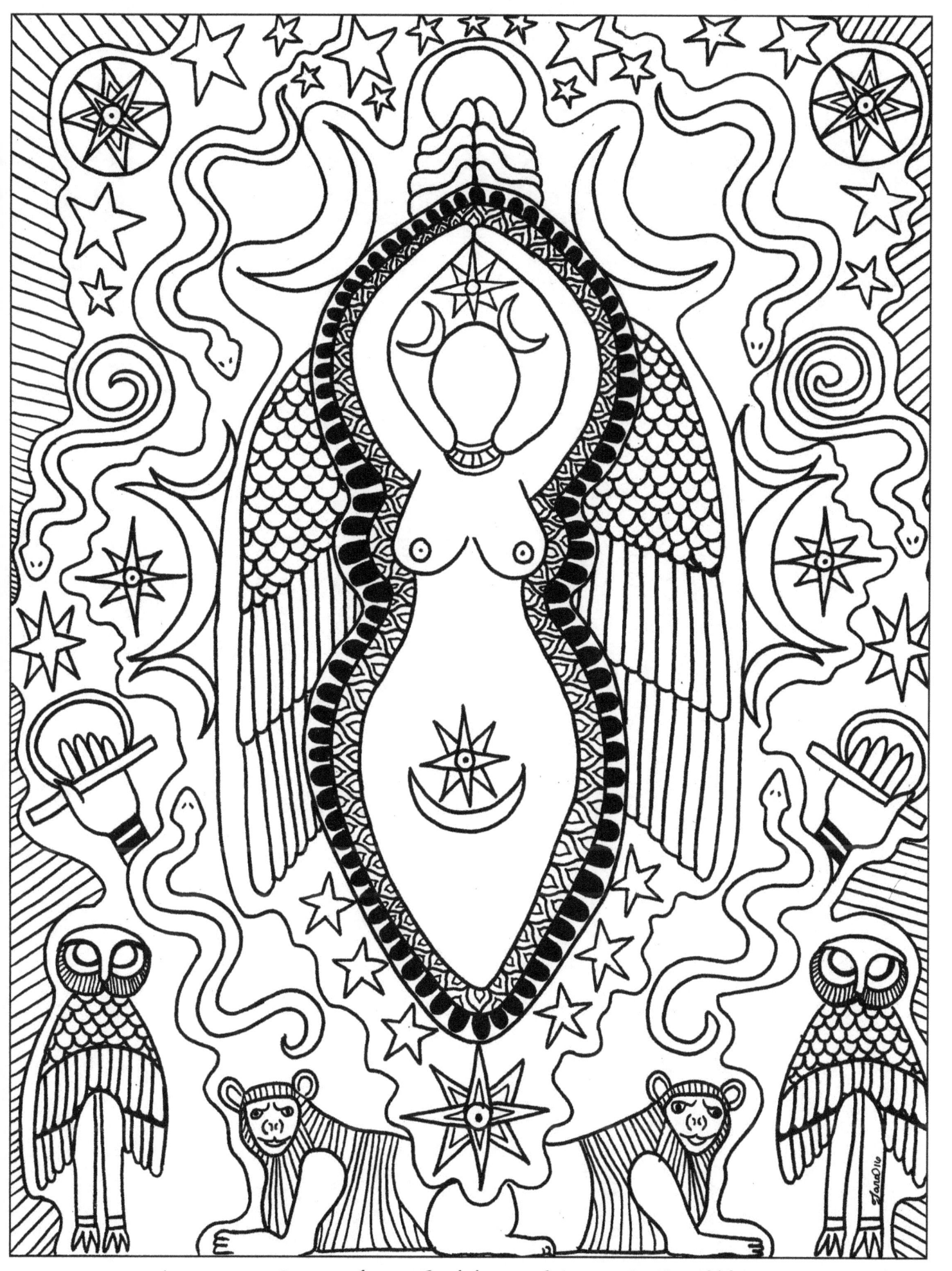

Inanna, Sumerian Goddess of Love & Fertility

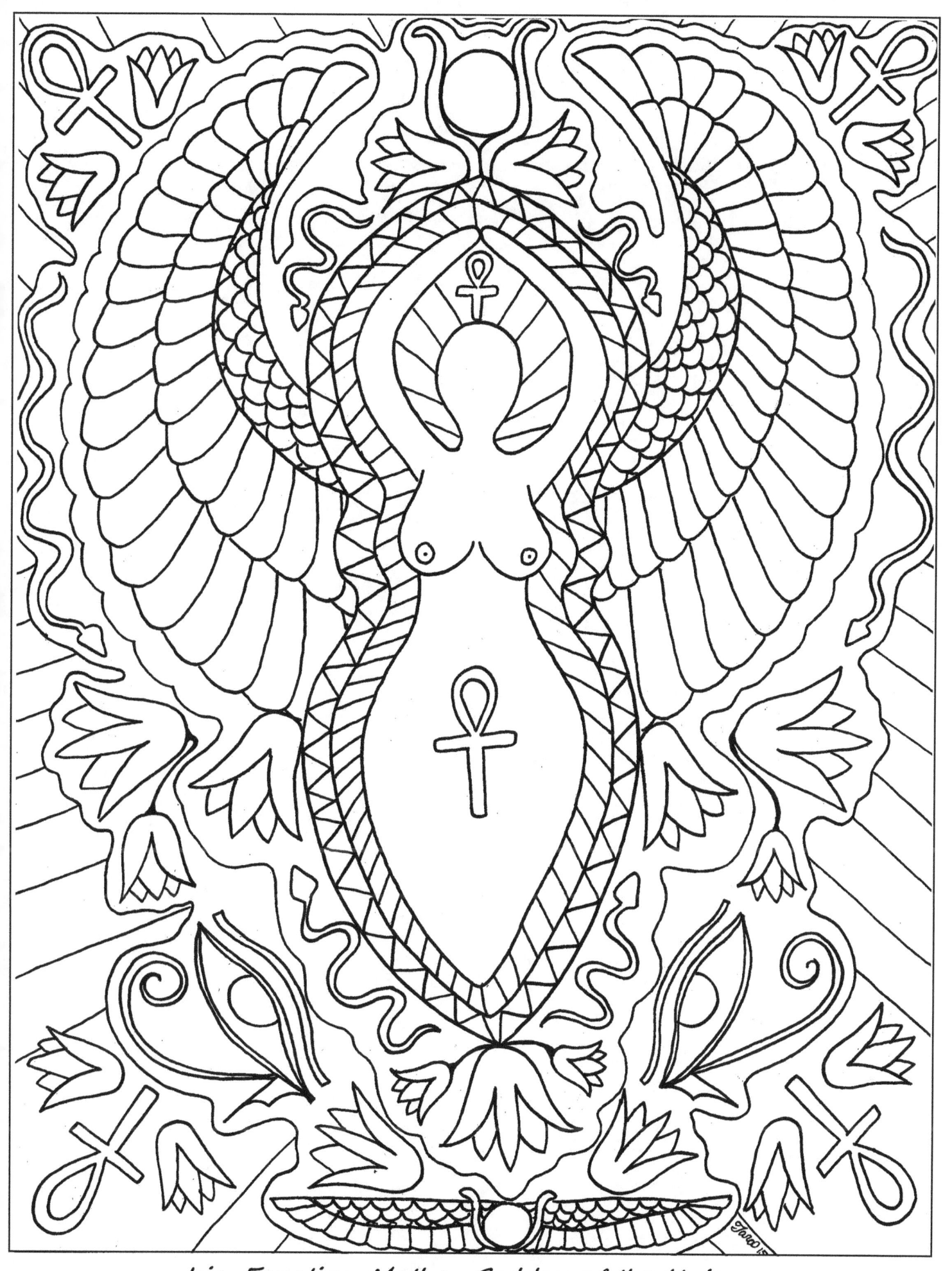

Isis, Egyptian Mother Goddess of the Universe

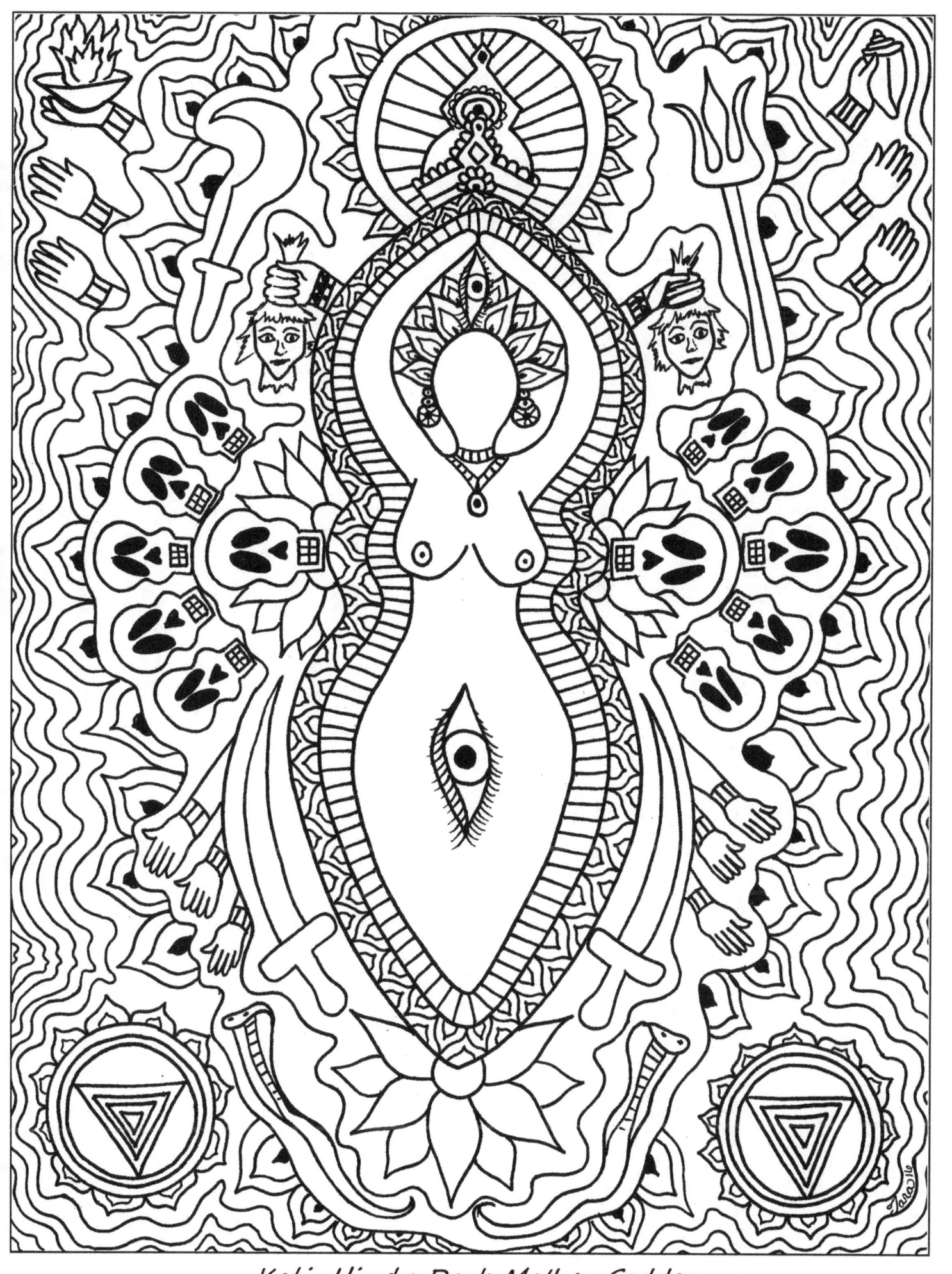

Kali, Hindu Dark Mother Goddess

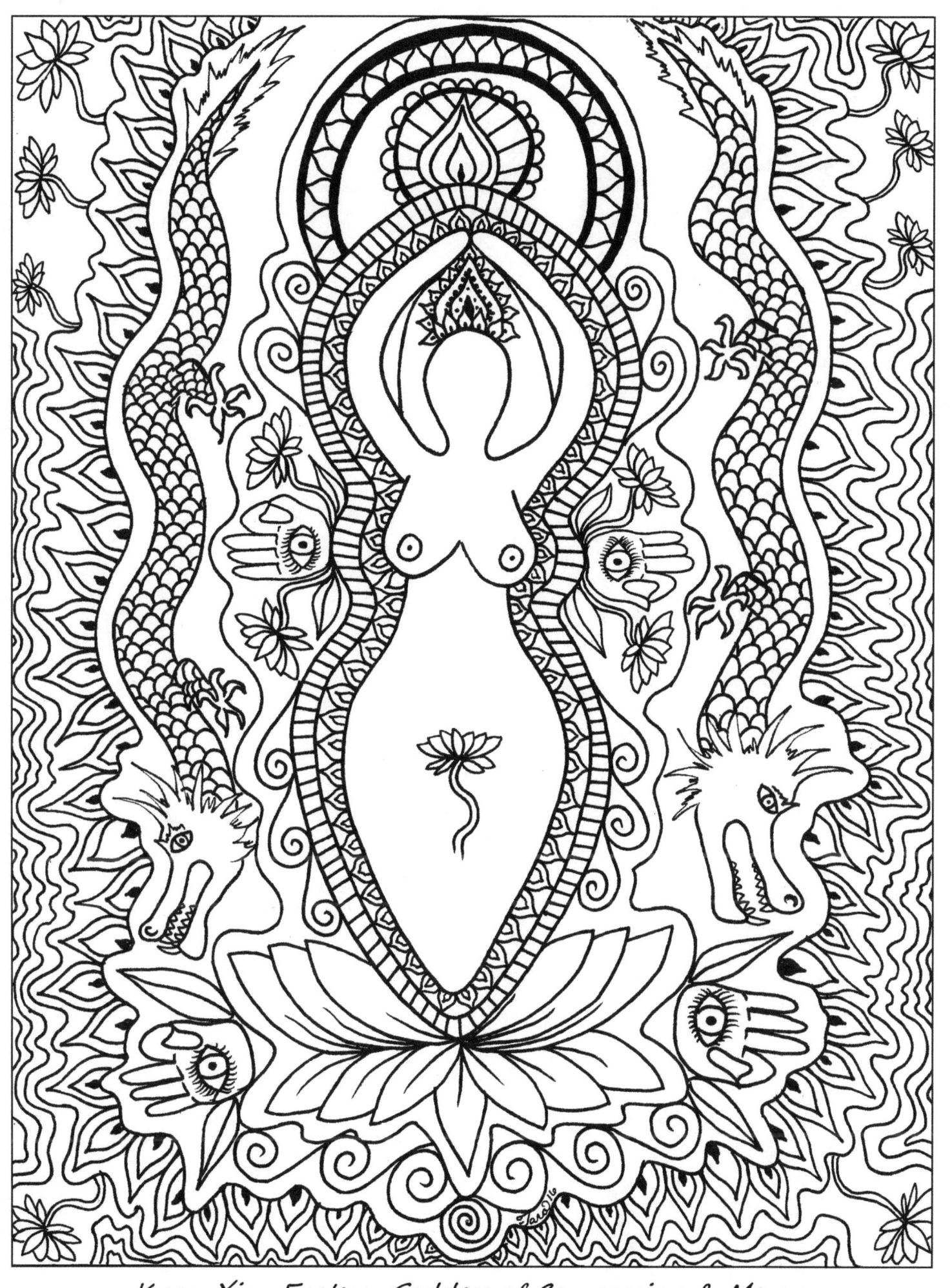

Kuan Yin, Eastern Goddess of Compassion & Mercy

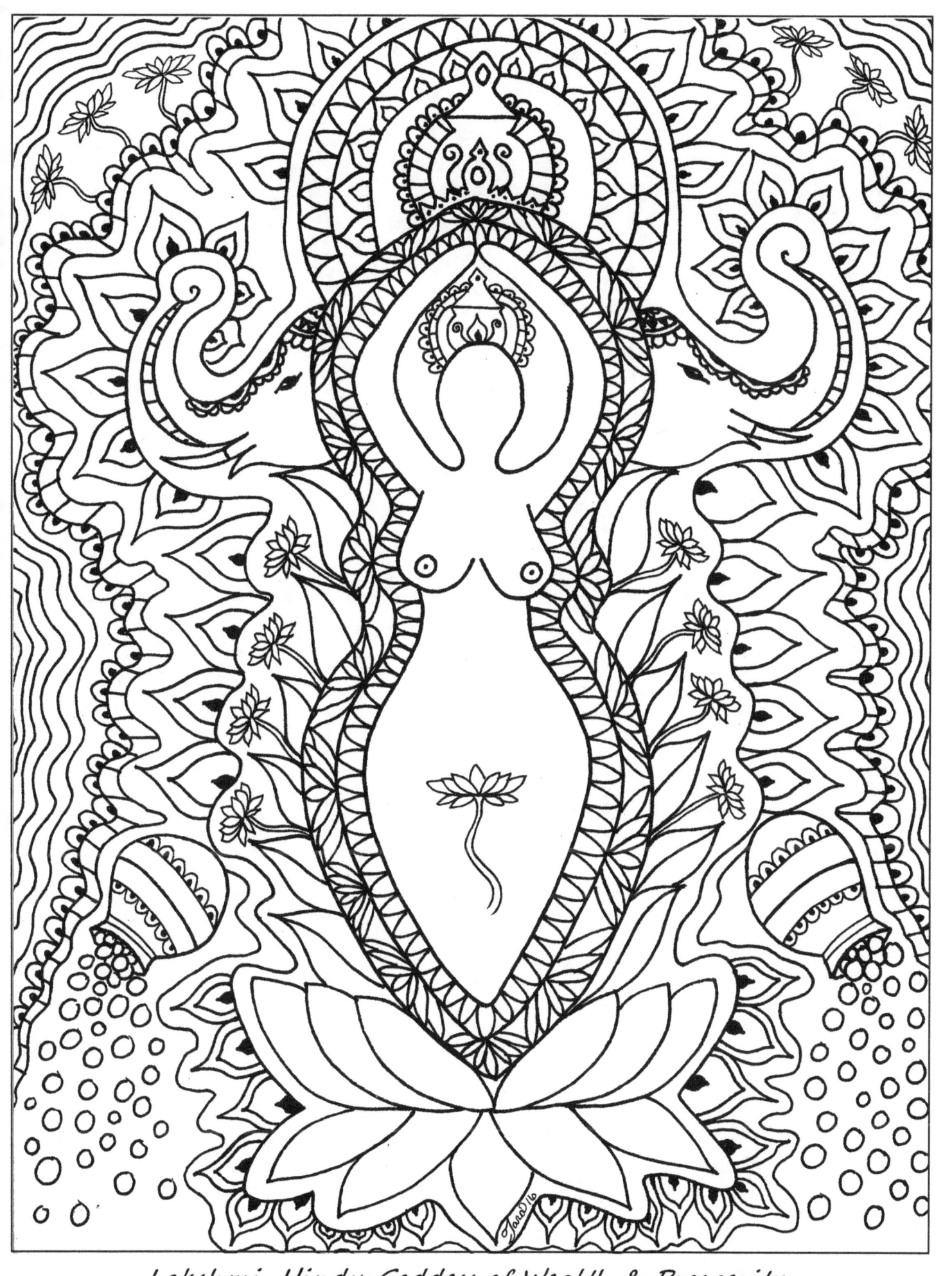

Lakshmi, Hindu Goddess of Wealth & Prosperity

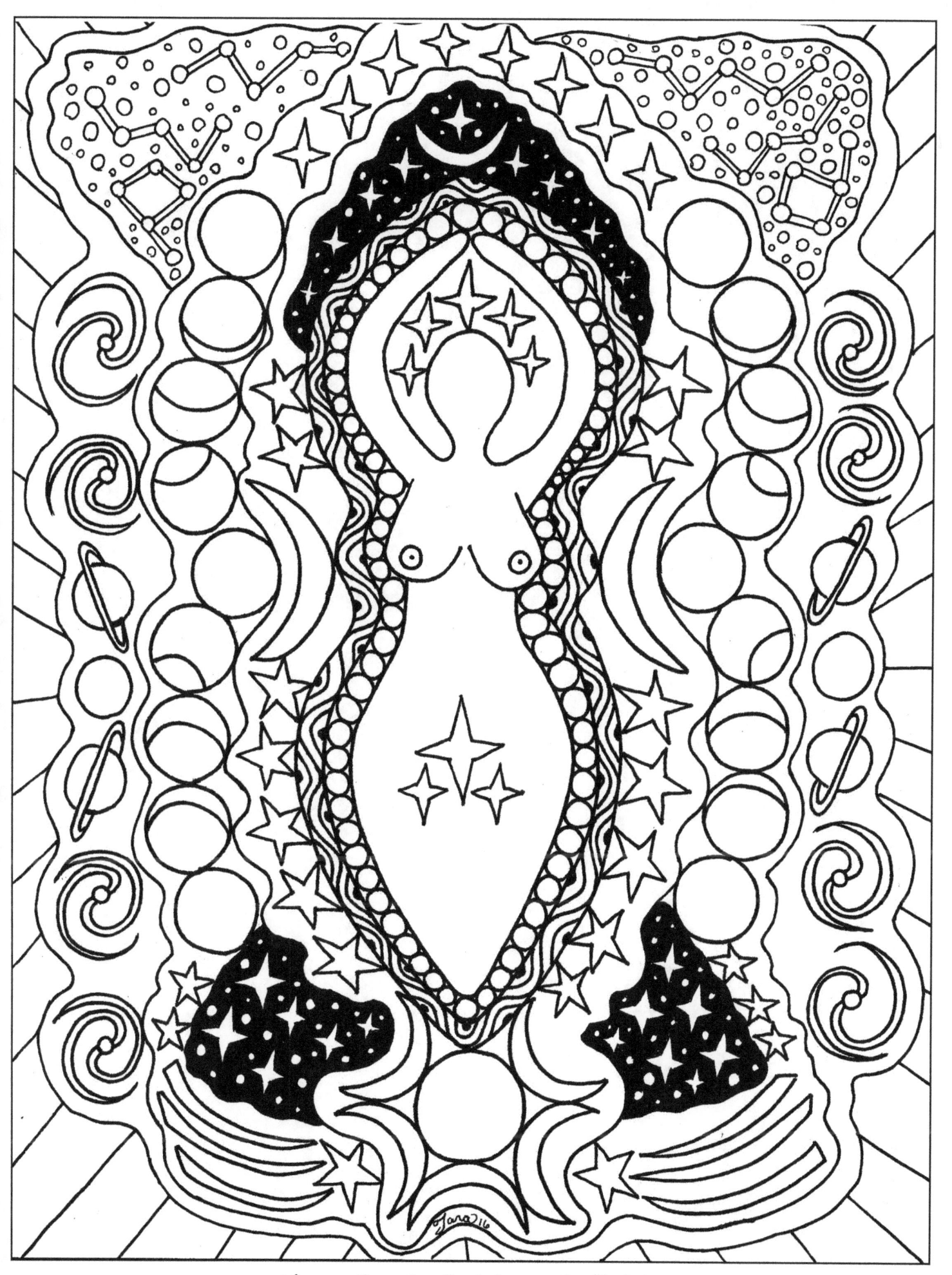

Nyx, Greek Goddess of Night

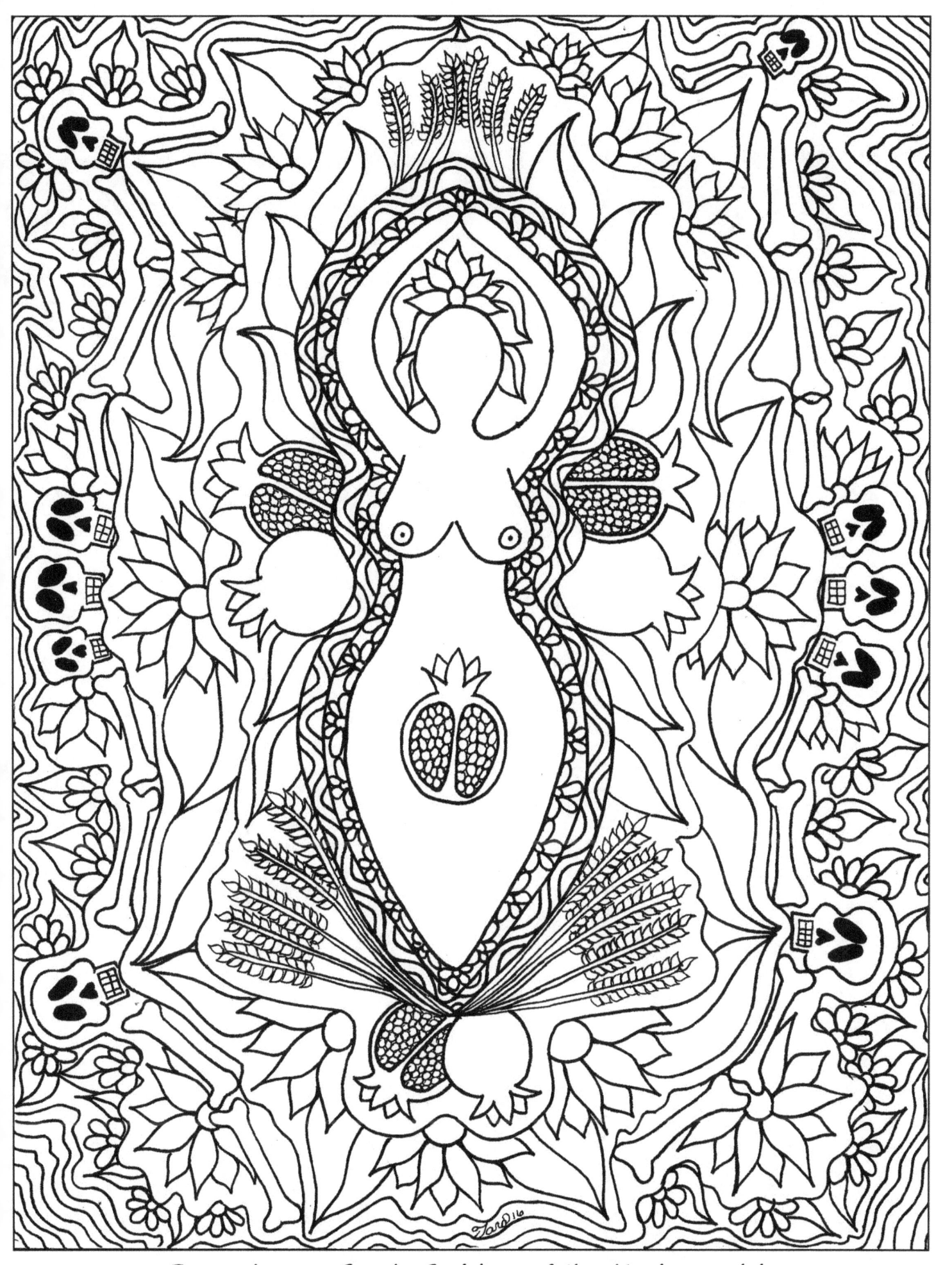

Persephone, Greek Goddess of the Underworld

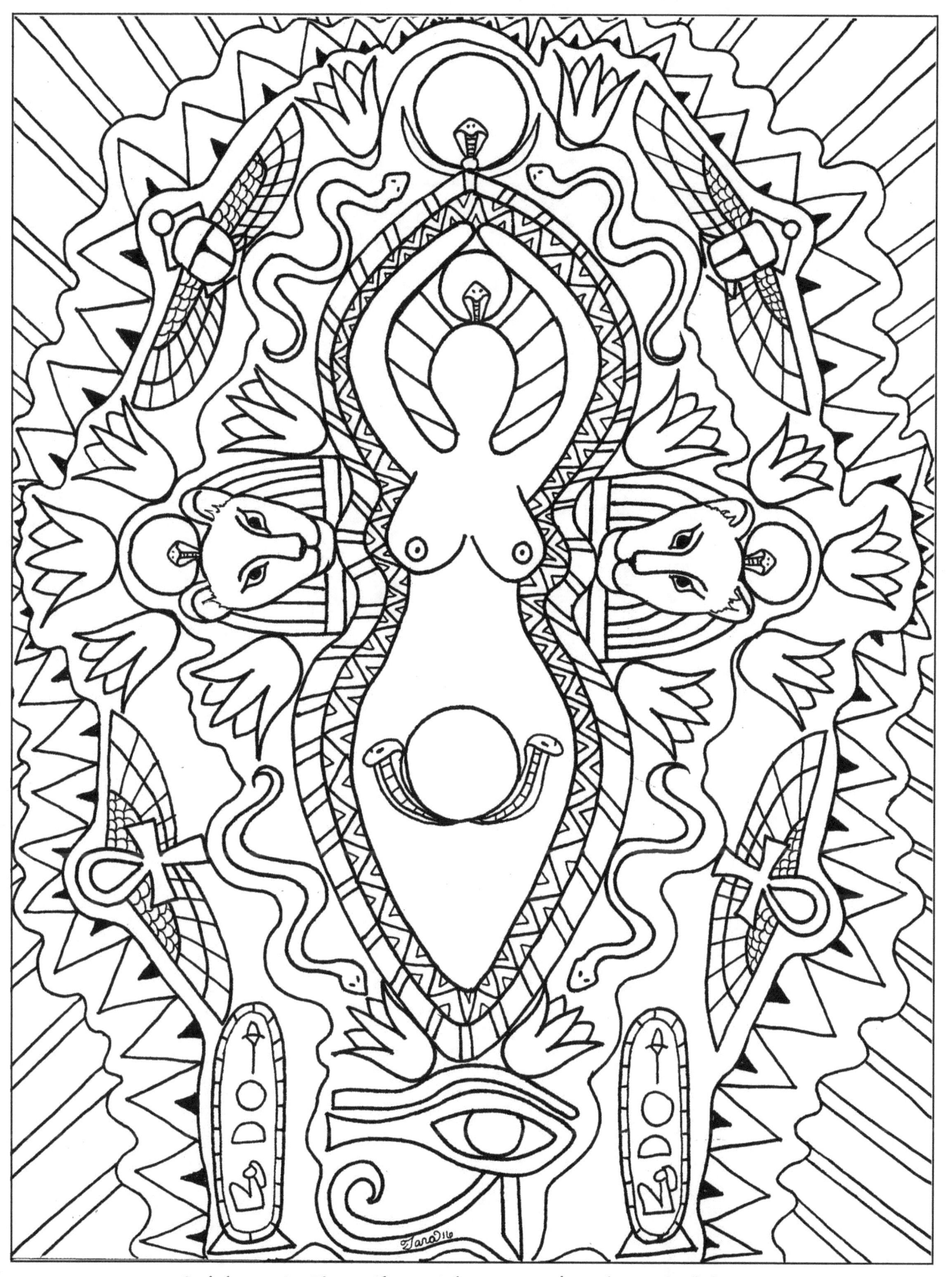

Sekhmet, Egyptian Lioness Warrior Goddess

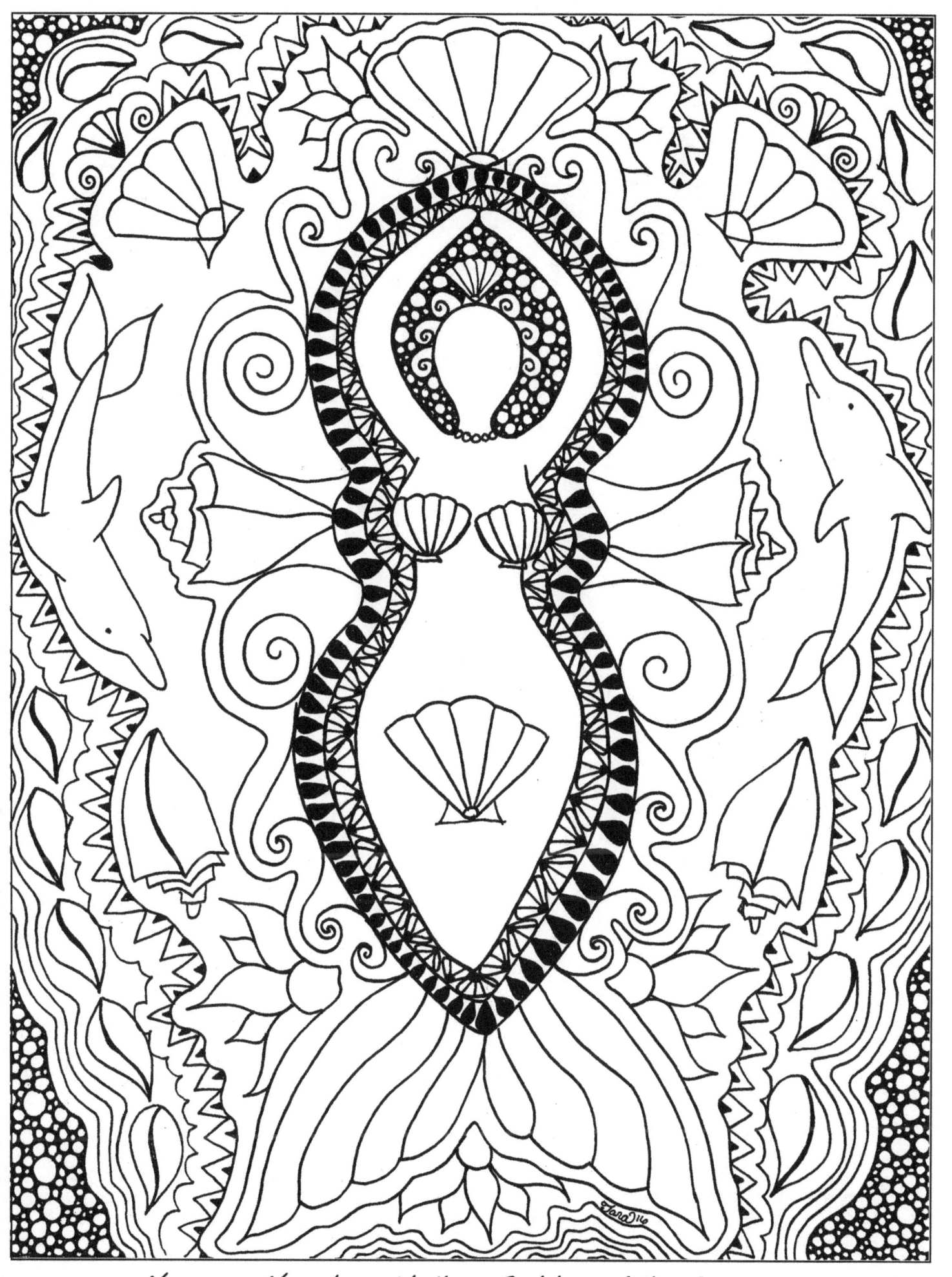

Yemaya, Yoruban Mother Goddess of the Ocean

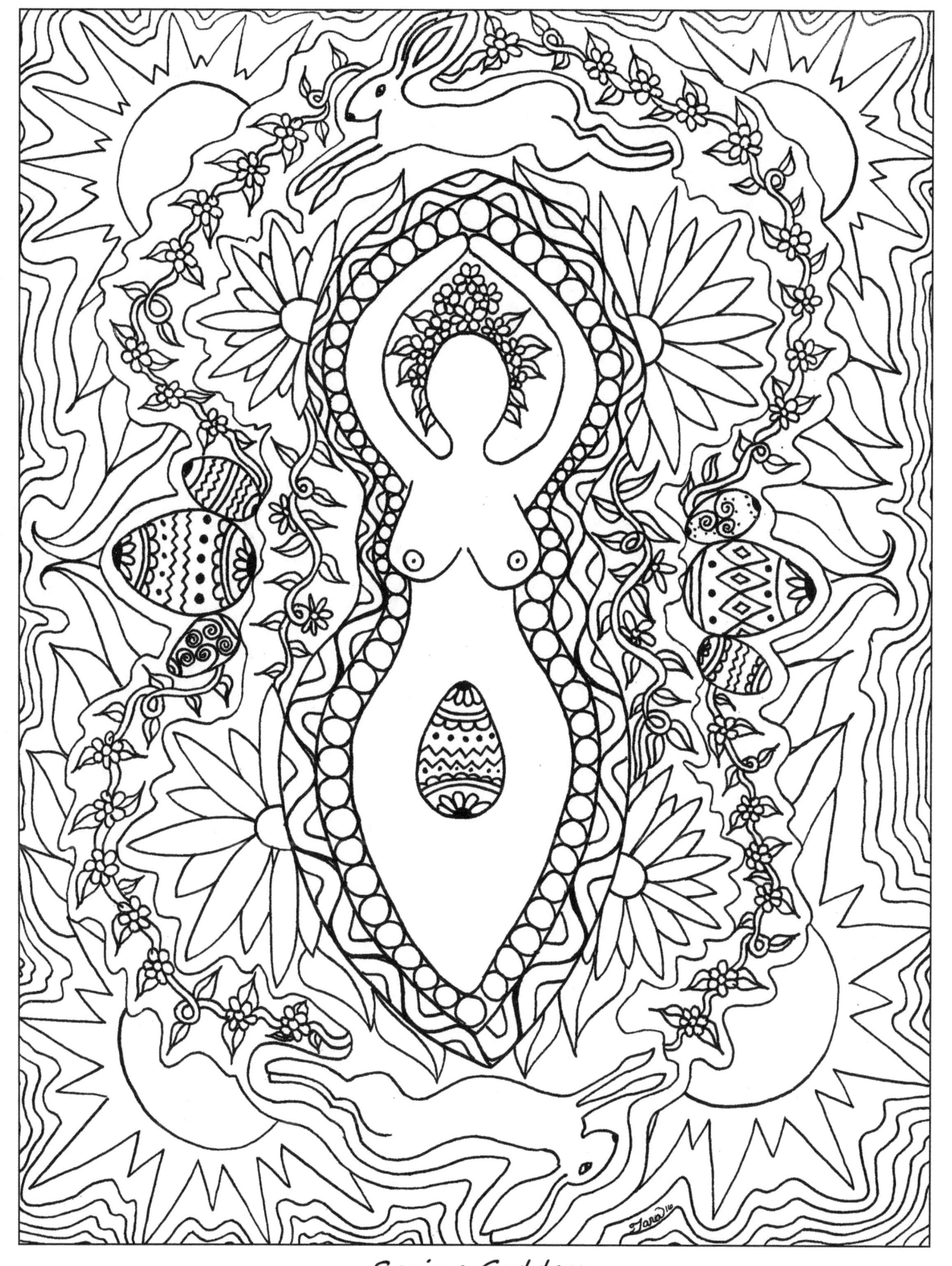

Spring Goddess

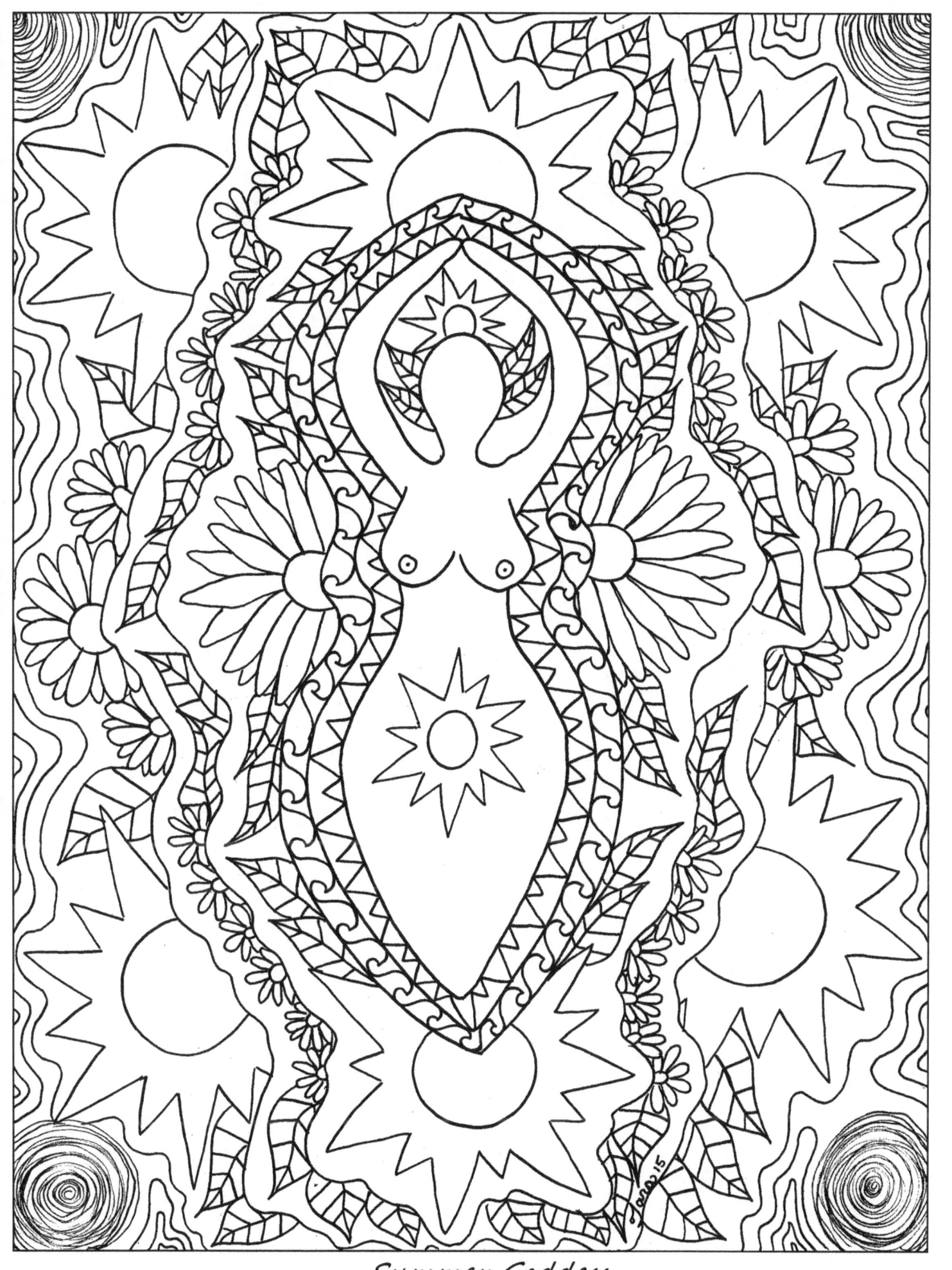

Summer Goddess

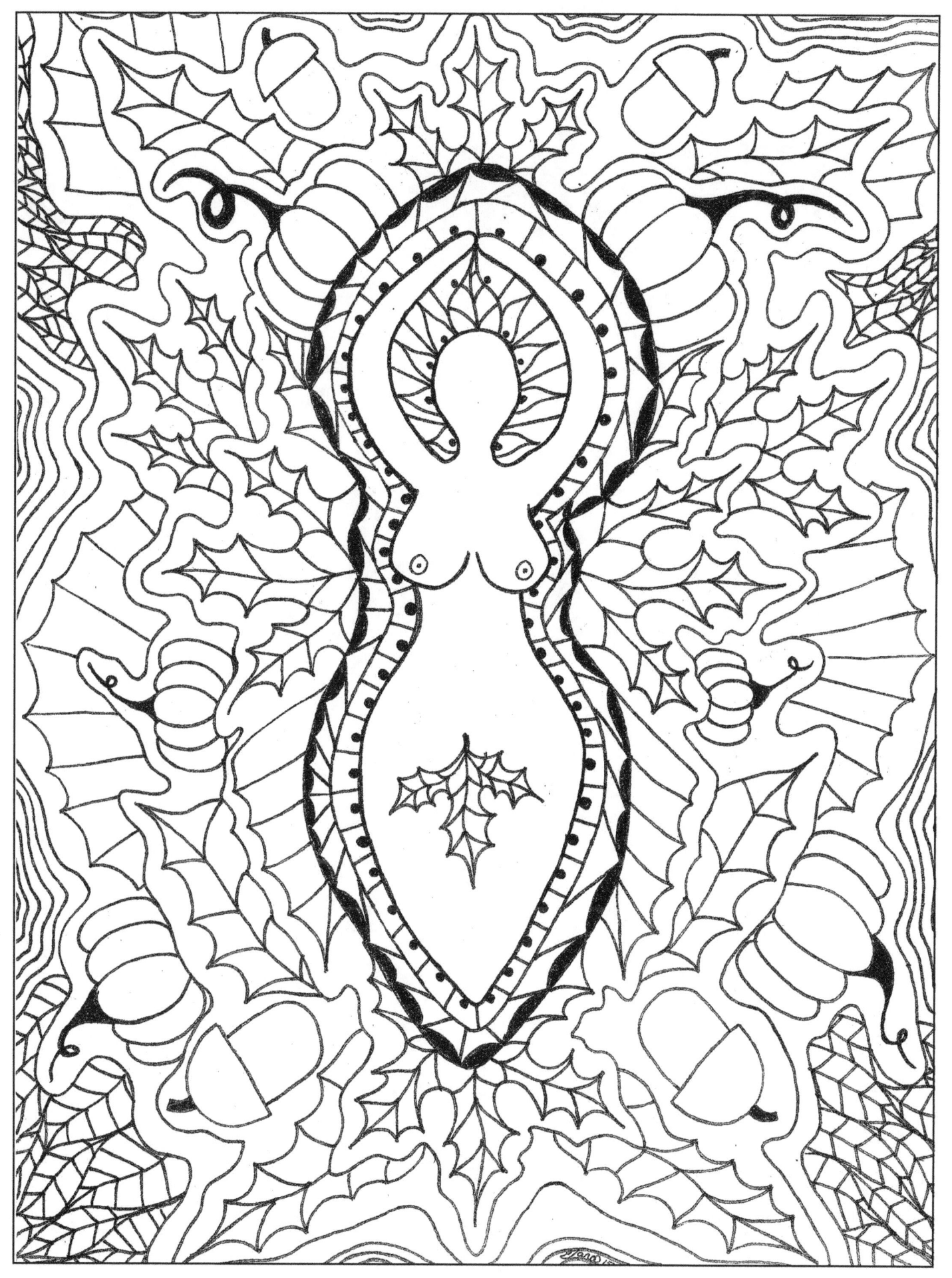

Autumn Goddess

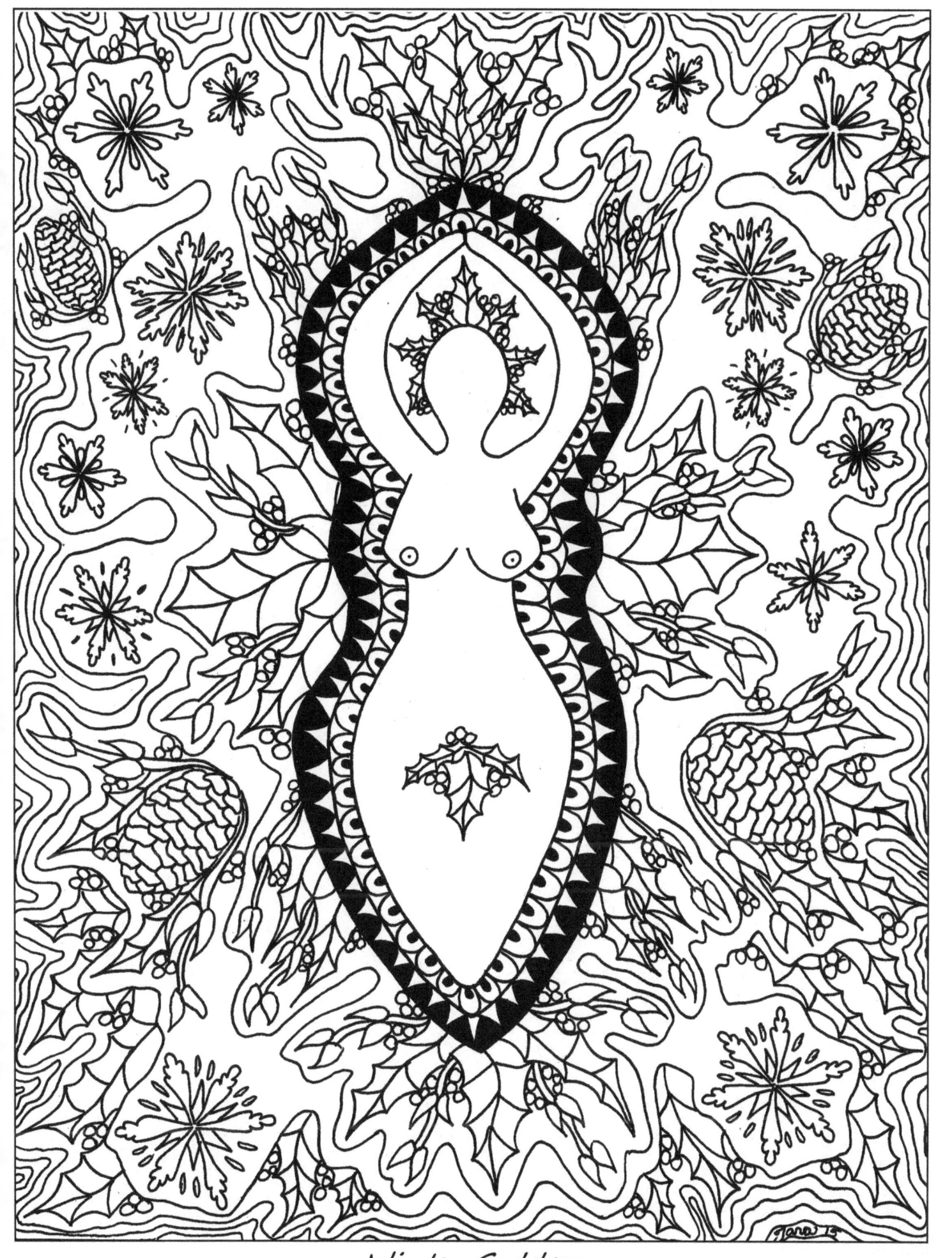

Winter Goddess